Advent Adventures

simple sketches for the advent season

by Susan M Brown

Scottish
Christian PRESS

First published in Great Britain
In 2003 by Scottish Christian Press
21 Young Street
Edinburgh EH2 4HU

Performing and Copying:

these books are designed to provide resources mainly for churches and amateur groups that want to use drama in worship, study and mission. **You are free to perform any of these plays and sketches and do not need permission, but we would appreciate receiving news of any productions. Our plays are protected by copyright and so we ask that you buy copies for each actor when you purchase one.** We hope that you will find them useful for the work of the Kingdom.

Fees for performances by professional companies will be subject to negotiation.

ISBN 1904325122

Cover illustration by Iain Campbell

Typeset by Heather Macpherson
Printed and bound in the UK by Bookchase UK Ltd

I want to live and work for Jesus
My saviour and my King
I want to live and work for Jesus
To me he's everything
I want to live and work for Jesus
My saviour and my King
For he died tomake more roly/me happy ~
And I swe him everything

Contents

These Scripts are dedicated to the Bright Sparks at Killearnan and to Stuart and all the other young people who have passed through the Youth Group at Dornoch.

Introduction

These scripts were written as part of the build up to Christmas and have all been 'performed' in Killearnan Parish Church on the Black Isle (a rural charge), or in Dornoch Cathedral. Sometimes it's been adults who have taken on the various roles, more often it's been members of the Youth Group.

Each script contains four sections, since we were in the practice of carrying them out in weekly 'episodes' over the four weeks of the advent services; but don't let this constrain you; each script can easily be done as one play - or, with a minimum of bother, adapted to a different number of 'episodes'!

Since the scripts were written from week to week, there was not a great deal of time for detailed preparation and those who participated tended to do so 'script in hand' and with minimum props and costumes. The plays formed part of the morning services during Advent and usually replaced the children's talk. There is, however, scope for using them in different settings at different times. They could be used all in one go, for example, with carols and readings in between - again in church, or in school, at guild meetings - wherever people of any age gather. Because these were originally written for our own use and location, we included lots of local references; so when putting them together for publication, I had to decide whether to take out all of these or not... But I felt they helped the flow of the narrative, and helped to indicate how to make the script more 'alive' to your own audience; so we decided to leave these in, to show how they worked for us. So you'll see throughout these scripts some local references, just as we used them, but which can and should be altered to suit your own location - to help with this, we've highlighted these with some footnoted suggestions as to how to adapt them.

Perhaps one other note of explanation is required before you read on. You will notice that in most of the plays there is a special role for the 'Star'. Now, in our own productions, this role ended up being played by the same person each year. Stuart's debut as The Star began when he was a mere 12 year old and his reputation has grown for five years. The people wait for him to appear and, when he does and says his usual 'Shine, shine', the place erupts! Everyone

1

cheers - including his fellow actors! Now he's a 6'3" young man and, because I don't want to push my luck, the latest Advent Script - Jesus Christ and the Stable of Promise - has been written without his starring role - however that can easily be changed...

With these few suggestions, I hope you can see how you can adopt and adapt these 'simple scripts' to your own personal needs and situation. Above all, I hope you get as much enjoyment – and inspiration - out of the experience as we did.

I'd just like to say thank you to Gill Cloke from SCP and her editor Sharon Jacobs, for encouraging me to work on the plays and for helping to make them more universally applicable - and for enduring my poor punctuation and grammar!

Susan Brown

MacChristmas MacArchers

Characters:

Narrator
Joe MacGrundy
Eddie MacGrundy
Joseph
Mary
Wise man 1
Wise man 2
Wise man 3
Heidyin from Ministry
Bystander

PART ONE

Scene note: *The 'Barn' (a few bales of hay, pitchfork, etc, or this can be just a sign suggesting) should be at the centre front of the audience. In each part of this play the three sets of characters move slowly further up the three aisles (or gangways) to the Barn, MacGrundys on the left, Mary and Joseph up the centre and the Wise Men on the right. Before and between their scenes they could sit amongst the audience.*

Narrator   Welcome to the first of four episodes coming to you live from down on the farm, Sutherland[1] style. Here the MacArcher family have successfully farmed for centuries and the neighbouring MacGrundys have done a little bit of this and a little bit of that...

    Scene: *MacGrundy farm. Joe and Eddie at back left of audience.*

---

1 Or use some local, or well-known, farming area

3

Joe	Aye, that's right enough - we MacGrundys have been here every bit as long as them MacArchers - haven't we Eddie?
Eddie	So you keep saying, Dad.
Joe	They wouldn't be the farmers they are today if it wasn't for the help we give them.
Eddie	Aye, we're so bad we help them to look good! Do you remember that night Phil MacArcher asked us to help him bring his sheep in so he could take them to the sales? We even managed to foul up on that one...
Joe	What do you mean we fouled up - there wasn't a chicken in sight!
Eddie	Dad! You know what I mean. Mind you we did have a good excuse, didn't we? Phil had sent us up to the top of Birichen2 - it was freezing cold and pitch black by the time we got there. We were just getting the flasks out when all of a sudden we saw these amazing lights!
Joe	*You* saw some lights you mean, and tried to tell me it was probably Rory boring Alice - in my day we tried to impress our girlfriends, not bore them!
Eddie	Aw Dad! The aurora borealis - the Northern Lights! I thought it was the Northern Lights! Except it wasn't, was it? Because then we heard voices...
Joe	Yeah, I remember wondering what the missus had put in the tea - and could I have some more...
Eddie	*(Exasperated)* It was angels, singing, telling us they had some good news. We were to leave Phil's sheep and go down into the village where we'd find a special baby...

2 Or name a well known high mountain or hill

4

Joe	And we got up straightaway and went, didn't we?
Eddie	I did but you took some persuading - if I remember rightly, it cost me the rest of the flask...
	Joe and Eddie stop moving, Mary and Joseph, begin moving forwards very slowly down the central aisle.
Joseph	Mary, I believe you... I think... but what on earth is my mother going to say? What's worse, what's yours going to do? To me?
Mary	I know it's not an easy thing for you to get your head round, Joseph. I know it must sound a bit far-fetched - but maybe it would help if we went away for a bit. We need to go north anyway to sort out some family business, why don't we give it all some time?
Joseph	Some time? Can you imagine what'll happen when this gets out? Can you imagine the nods and the winks at the dance next month - he's the bloke whose wife's pregnant by God - by God, is that right? Ha, ha, ha! Mary, Mary, Mary... what's going on?
Narrator	What is going on? Will Joseph and Mary head north? Will they avoid the wrath of Mary's mother? Will Joe and Eddie just blame the tea and go back to Eddie's wife for more - or will they make it to the village? Find out in the next episode of the MacArchers, same time, same place, next week.

PART TWO

Narrator	In last week's MacArchers, we left Mary and Joseph heading north. Joe and Eddie heading for the village. And Phil MacArcher footing the bill...

Mary and Joseph, having moved a little way to the front down the central aisle, mime climbing into a train carriage with bags.

Mary	I know I said maybe we should try and look as though we'd been married for a while, but there's no need to make me carry *all* the cases...
Joseph	It's taking longer to travel north than I thought it would - this camel-train is two days late!
Mary	They said there's wet sand on the line.
Joseph	...and the buffet car gives a new meaning to the phrase 'eating on the hoof.'
Mary	Joseph... Do you think this was sensible - coming all this way, I mean. The baby could come at any time and I don't think the Burghfield[3] accepts luncheon vouchers.
Joseph	Don't worry Mary - we'll find some place... if we ever get there!

Mary and Joseph stop, Joe and Eddie, on the left, start moving again.

Eddie	Come on, Dad, keep going. I've half a mind to go on without you.
Joe	If you'd half a mind, we wouldn't be doing this at all...bright lights... angels... singing... *(Looking at a flask he's carrying)* Maybe I need to put more water in it...

3 Or name a local pub/restaurant.

6

Joe and Eddie stop moving forwards, Heidyin from Ministry with clipboard and three wise men enter rear right.

Heidyin   Right gentlemen, we have evidence here at the Ministry of Agriculture of a severe case of BSE (Blokes Seein' Engles) in Birichen[4] and I would like to send you three wise and sensible men to investigate. Your instructions are as follows: there is a bright star shining - follow it. Is that understood?

3 wise men   Yes sir!

Man   Off you go then chaps and... good luck!

All rise and shake hands.

Narrator   Will the wise men from the ministry see the bright light? How long can it take Joe and Eddie to reach the village? Will Mary and Joseph find a welcome inn at the Burghfield[5]? Join us again next week, for the next exciting episode of The MacArchers.

PART THREE

Narrator   The Wise Men from the Ministry of Agriculture are following the star. Joe and Eddie MacGrundy are following the angels' instructions - and poor Mary and Joseph are looking for somewhere to stay.

Mary and Joseph nearly at the front in the central aisle.

Mary   I think we need to find somewhere quick.

Joseph   You know as well as I do there's just nowhere with any room.

4 Or name a well-known high mountain or hill.
5 Or name a local pub/restaurant.

7

Mary	Joseph, I mean *quick*!
Joseph	I'm doing everything I can, I just don't know what to do next!
Mary	I don't think there's much time...
Joseph	Look, I'll ask this guy.
	Turns to Bystander - in pew
	Excuse me sir, but have you any idea where we could get a room for the night?
Bystander	*(Still sitting in pew)* It just so happens I run a nice wee hotel, just over the bridge in Dornoch[6] - in the town itself...
Joseph	Great! Can we have a room for the night?
Bystander	For tonight?
Joseph	Yes please - my wife really needs a bed.
Bystander	Tonight?
Joseph	Yes, tonight!
Bystander	I'm sorry lad, we're so popular bookings have to be made way in advance - and this weekend things are so hectic I've even let my own children's' rooms!
Joseph	*(Disappointed)* Oh..
Mary	Please help us. Please. We're getting desperate.
Bystander	I'll tell you what I can do, I can give you the barn - it's not much, I know, but it's wind and water-tight and the Missus mucked it out only this morning...

6 Or use the local suburb or town name.

Joseph	Dung! I mean, done - lead us to it!

Mary and Joseph move to centre front of audience, Three Wise Men continue moving up the right hand aisle. Wise Man 1 is looking upward through binoculars.

W. Man 1	Aye, the nights are fair drawin' in.

Stops looking up, rubbing neck.

It gives you a crick in the neck.

W. Man 2	What does?
W. Man 1	Star-gazing!
W. Man 3	Is this going to take long, do you think - only my wife doesn't like me doing nights.
W. Man 1	It'll take the length of time it takes.
W. Man 3	I wouldn't complain normally, you know, it's just that I catch my death of cold so easily and I only have one clean hanky.
W. Man 1	I think it's stopped.
W. Man 3	Well, I did blow it just a moment ago - but it'll start again, you wait and see - noses run in our family.

Other wise men look at him incredulously.

W. Man 2	(Checking script) It does say wise men here, doesn't it?
W. Man 1	I think *the star* has stopped. Yes, I'm sure it has. Come on men, let's go!

9

Narrator	As the three Wise Men set off into the sunset, we leave this week's episode of the MacArchers. Where have Joe and Eddie got to? How did Joseph and Mary find the barn? Did they make it in time? Your answers on a postcard please, and look out for the final episode in our epic tale next week…

PART FOUR

Narrator	Things have reached fever pitch here in the 'Cambridge of the north'7. Mary and Joseph are settled in the barn with their new arrival and about to receive some unexpected visitors…
	Joe and Eddie arrive outside the barn - front of church where Mary and Joseph are - arguing.
Joe	Eddie I'm telling you, I'm not going in first - this was your stupid idea - you were the one who saw the bright lights and heard them angels - *you* go in.
Eddie	Dad, you're the oldest, it would look better if you went first - that way if we've made a fool of ourselves we could just blame your age, say you're wandering a wee bit these days…
Joe	There's nothing wrong with *my* head - it's *yours* that needs looking at.
	Joseph approaches.
Joseph	Can I help you gentlemen?
Joe	*(Removing cap)* Good evening sir, my simple son and I were just out for a walk and we thought… Eh…we thought, we'd just… eh…

7 Or use the nick-name for the local suburb or town.

Nudges Eddie.

Eddie   Actually we were told to come here, by an angel - well, a whole company of angels actually, they said that today in this town, a saviour would be born.

Joseph   Come in then, friends, come in and see him for yourselves...

All sit and admire the infant. Wise men stop outside the barn, arguing.

W. Man 1 This is it. This is where the star stops. Let's go in.

W. Man 3 Do you think we should? There might be all sorts of germs in there.

W. Man 2 *(Firmly)* You heard what the man said, let's go!

Three Wise Men barge confidently in and then stop short. Wise men 1 and 2 fall to their knees, 3 stays standing, they grab him and pull him down as well.

W. Man 1 He's so perfect!

W. Man 2 Beautiful!

W. Man 3 *(Talking to himself, searching his pockets)* What can I give him? I've only got these forms from the Ministry with me... I know, my gold pen *(Pulls out pen and looks at it)* My wife will kill me - but so what! *(Hands it over, smiling)*

W. Man 2 *(To Joseph)* He'll need this. *(Hands over paper)*

Joseph   What's this?

W. Man 2 His own milk quota[8].

---

8 In a non-farming community, substitute a locally prized official dooket - e.g. parking permit, building warrant, local supermarket vouchers!...

11

W. Man 1   *(Embarrassed)* I don't have anything to give him... Unless...
           Do you think he'd like this...

           Takes off his coat.

Narrator   *(Whispering)* There, I think we'll leave things. But this baby
           came, not to stay a baby; he came... to grow up. Listen out
           over the next few weeks and years, and you'll hear some
           more of his story - a story which goes on right up to this
           present day... and beyond.

A Stable Big Brother

Characters:

Voice 1 / Gold
Voice 2 / Frank
Voice 3 / Incense
Voice 4 / Mary
Voice 5 / Myrrh
Voice 6 / Joseph
Voice 7 / Star
Narrator
'Host' of Angels - at least three
three Boys/three Shepherds
three Girls/three Wise Men
Davina (Big Brother compere)
Innkeeper

Sound effects:

Big Brother theme tune
Drum-roll

PART ONE

Voice 1	Have you heard the latest? We're doing an Advent play!
Voice 2	What? With tea-towels over the head and dressing gowns and all the rest?
Voice 3	A bit more up-to-date than that. Christmas... soap style...
Voice 1	What, you mean like - 'the Far Eastenders'?...
Voice 3	Mm, bit 'Far out'...

Voice 1	Well then, 'the MacArchers'?...
Voice 3	Naw, that's old hat!...
Voice 2	What other soap can we serialise over 4 weeks?
Voice 1	Maybe it'll be Incarnation Street...
Voice 2	In car what?
Voice 1	Incarnation - that's the name for God becoming human.
Voice 2	*(Yawning)* Well, you learn something new every day...
Voice 3	Or maybe we could go for something trendy like 'Friends' and base our advent adventure on that!
Voice 4	Yeah - that would be a good one... The shepherd friends and the star-gazing friends and their journey to find the baby - yep - I think that one's got potential.
Voice 5	Or maybe, 'Haywatch' - since Jesus was born in a stable...
	All Groan...
Voice 4	We could use 'Home and Away' - we wouldn't need to change the title...
Voice 2	Sounds like a football fixture list.
Voice 6	*(Coming in)* Let me put you out of your misery guys, here it is, this year's advent script.
Voice 1	'A Christmas Big Brother'!
	Play Big Brother theme tune.

Voice 2	But Jesus was just a baby…
Voice 1	Wait, you're right, that's been scored out. It's 'A Christmas Wee Brother'.
Voice 3	How on earth are we going to do that?
Voice 1	The usual parts - 3 shepherds…
Three boys	No problem, we'll do that.
Voice 1	A few wise men…
Voice 2	We'll need really good actors for that.
Three girls	Then maybe the girls should play those parts.
Voice 1	We need a Mary and a Joseph…
Voice 4	I'll be Mary.
Voice 6	I'll be Joseph - as long as there's no kissing.
Voice 5	What version of the Christmas story have *you* read?
Joseph/V6	Only joking!
Voice 1	We need an innkeeper and a host of angels…
All left	We'll cover those parts.
Voice 1	That just leaves…
Voice 7	Me! It leaves me.
Joseph/V6	Well, you're a bit big for the baby Jesus…

Voice 5	You're not joking!
Joseph	I don't think you'd fit in the crib…
Voice 3	*I know!…*
	Voice 3 gets everyone into a huddle and whispers… People go 'yeah' 'cool!.' 'excellent' etc.
Voice 7	Come on guys, what's going on?
	Huddle breaks up.
Voice 3	We've got the perfect part for you… a-one, a-two, a-one two three…
All	*(Chanting)* You're a star, you're a star… shining bright and a way, way far…
Voice 7	Thanks a lot!
Mary/V4	Seriously, it's an important role - without you there would be no wise men…
Star/V7	Okay, I'll do it - just don't sing any more.
Joseph	But listen, what's all this got to do with Big Brother - where's nasty Nick, the wonderful Craig, that nice Anna and all the rest?[1]
Voice 1	Ah well, this is going to be Big Brother-…
Voice 2	*(interrupts)* - Wee Brother!

1 Substitute names for any of the latest Big Brother characters.

Voice 1	- This is going to be *Wee Brother*, with a difference. We don't need nasty Nick, people will vote out the characters in the story - oops we've got two minutes until the end of this week's programme, you'd better get to your positions and start impressing the audience…

Immediate hubbub - Angels start singing 'Alleluia' off-key, the star shouts 'Shine, shine', the shepherds shout 'Baa-baa', the wise men point furiously to the sky shouting 'Follow that star.'

Narrator	Who will be voted out of the stable first? The off-key angels? The star?

All	(*Chant*) He's a star, he's a star, shining bright and a way, way far.

Narrator	The shepherds, or the wise men - or perhaps it might be Mary and Joseph? For the results of our *straw* poll, come back to the stable next week, same time, same place.

PART TWO

Narrator	Welcome to this week's episode of Big Brother…

Joseph	Wee Brother, you mean.

Narrator	Welcome to this week's episode of Wee Brother. You're about to discover who, after last week's scintillating performance, is to be thrown out of the Wee Brother stable. Will it be the shepherds?

Shepherds	(*all over-acting furiously*) Baa!

Narrator	The wise men?

Wise men	(*All point and shout keenly*) Follow that star.

Narrator	The off-key angels…
Angels	*(Enthusiastic off-key singing)* Alleluia!
Narrator	… or the star?
All	*(Chant)* He's a star, he's a star, shining bright and a way, way far.
Narrator	Or perhaps even Mary and Joseph!
All	*(Gasp with horror)*
Davina	Hello, Wee Brother stable, this is Davina![2] And… the first people nominated to leave the Wee Brother stable are… *(Drum roll)* The Shepherds! You have one minute to say goodbye.

Everyone runs to hug them and then wave tearful goodbyes then gather in the middle again. Angels sneak off to hide in pulpit[3]. |
Voice 1	Wow! That's horrible. Waiting to see who's out.
Voice 2	It's like waiting outside the head teacher's door.
Mary	It's even worse than going to the dentist.
Voice 2	Who do you think will be next to go?
Joseph	Well, it can't be Mary and me.
Mary	Mary and *I* dear, Mary and I!
Joseph	It can't be *us* because, well, because, well, we're Jesus' parents, aren't we?

2 Or use the latest Big Brother Compere's name
3 Or somewhere else suitable in your location, where they can be visible but 'concealed'

Voice 3	Joseph, have you ever actually read the story?
Joseph	Course I have - my mum's forever going on about it.
Voice 3	Well then, you'll remember that Joseph's is only a bit part.
Mary	*(Smugly)* A supporting role - to moi.
	Wanders off to see what angels are up to, stays looking in at them, baby in arms.
Voice 3	He kind of just went along with things...
Joseph	But listen guys, I got her to Bethlehem. I found the stable. I made the crib for the baby. *(Turning to face star)* It's the *star* who should go...
All	*(Chant)* He's a star, he's a star, shining bright and a way, way far.
Joseph	He doesn't even *say* anything in the story, he just hangs there in the sky.
Star	'Scuse me - I didn't even want to *be* the star. *You* lot told me it was an important part. Without me there would be no wise men you said...
	Wise men start grinning nervously...
W. Man 1	Of course you're important.
W. Man 2	And we are too.
W. Man 3	The story needs us. Star *and* wise men.
W. men 1-3	Definitely!

Voice 2	So - who's out next then?
Mary	(*Running from angels' hiding place, holding paper and pencils*) Hey everybody, look at this! I found the angels with these!
	Angels try to look innocent.
Voice 3	Paper and pencils!
	Joseph runs up to them.
Joseph	And a mobile phone! (*Holds up a mobile*) The angels are trying to rig the voting!
Star	You cheats!
Davina	(*Voice off*) Hello Wee Brother stable, this is Davina.
	Everyone shushes everyone else...
	You knew the rules when you came in here. No paper or pens. No communication with the outside world. Angels, I'm afraid you're going to be the first to be *expelled* from the Wee Brother stable. Go now. Goodbye!
	Angels exit, crestfallen.
Voice 2	I suppose they're fallen angels now!..
Narrator	There, I'm afraid, we need to leave things for this week. Cast, you have the next 20 seconds to make an impression.
	Immediate hubbub - the Star shouts 'Shine shine', the Wise Men point furiously to the sky shouting 'Follow that star', Mary and Joseph smile beatifically and look saintly.

Narrator	You, the audience are asked to cast your vote and to come back next week, same time, same place, for the results of this, the second straw poll in the Wee Brother stable...

PART THREE

Narrator	Welcome to this, the third of our programmes coming to you live from the Wee Brother stable. Last week we witnessed the first people to be expelled from the stable, when the angels were caught cheating. The Shepherds had just been voted out by you. So who will be leaving the Wee Brother stable this week? The wise men?
Wise men	*(Point and shout)* Follow that star.
Narrator	The star itself?
Star:	*(Shout)* Shine, shine.
Narrator	Or Mary and Joseph!
All	*(Gasp with horror)*
Narrator	For the results of this, the latest straw poll in the Wee Brother stable - over to you, Davina...
Davina	Thank you. Well, you, the audience, have already decided who should go, the votes are cast. Let's get on and put the contestants out of their misery. Hello Wee Brother stable, this is Davina.
All	*(Mutters of 'hello', 'hi', much shuffling and nervous looks)*
Davina	The second nomination to leave the stable is for... Mary and Joseph. You have one minute to say goodbye.

The wise men and star go wild at staying in, then try to look sad for Mary and Joseph's sake.

21

Davina	We'll leave the wise men and the star in the stable as we talk to last week's shepherds and fallen angels, and perhaps we'll also get a chance to speak to the newly thrown-out young couple... Shepherds, if I can turn to you - why do you think you were the first to go?
Shepherd 1	They said they couldn't stand our bleating.
Shepherd 2	Baaa-aarmy if you ask me!
Shepherd 3	Meeeh-ntal!
Shepherd 2	They didn't like our washing habits either.
Davina	Your *washing* habits?
Shepherd 3	It's just our lifestyle - we do it when we can fit it in.
Shepherd 1	It's traditional.
Shepherd 2	Shepherds have *always* washed their socks by night!
Davina	And how about you angels - how have you been since your dramatic downfall?
Angel 1	Our halos have slipped!
	Holding up halos which are bent, as if they've been forced down over ears.
Angel 2	Our street cred has slipped too.
Angel 3	People used to put us up on top of their Christmas tree - now they're leaving us up in the loft!
Angel 1	All those centuries helping people, blown just like that!

Davina	Sorry to stop you there, but here come Mary and Joseph...
	Mary and Joseph move towards Davina.
	Mary! Joseph! What does it feel like to be the next weakest link?
	Fiddles with ear, as if listening on earpiece
	- Uh? Oh! Sorry wrong programme - what does it feel like to have been thrown out of the Wee Brother stable?
Mary	I'm just going to ponder these things in my heart.
Joseph	She does that a lot, you know.
Davina	You must be terribly disappointed.
Joseph	Oh we are, we are - we thought we were pretty central to things - it just shows you how wrong you can be.
Davina	Mary, what are you carrying under your coat?
Mary	It's the baby. We couldn't possibly leave him behind. Not on his own.
Joseph	Home alone - it's not allowed.
Mary	No Mary, no baby.
Joseph	No Mary, no *Joseph*, no baby.
Mary	No baby, no story.
Joseph	*(Turning to audience)* Are you sure you should have voted us out?

Star	Yeah, 'cos I'm the star.
All	*(Chant)* He's a star, he's a star, shine, shine!
Davina	Shepherds, angels, Mary and Joseph... Good bye!

They exit.

Wee Brother stable, hello.

All say 'hi' and look pleased with themselves.

Congratulations guys, you have made it through to week 3. How do you feel?

Voice 1	Pretty pleased actually.
Voice 2	It's always sad to see people go.
Voice 3	But it's great to know *we're* still here.
Voice 1-3	Yesss!
Voice 3	Quality. That's what it is.
Voice 2	Class.
Davina	So who is left in the stable?
Voice 1	The Wise Men.
Wise men	*(Point and shout)* Follow that star.
Voice 2	And the star.
All	*(Chant)* He's a star, he's a star, shine, shine!

Davina	So... Who are you?
Voice 5	Us?
Davina	Yes, you. If they're the wise men...
Wise men	*(Point and shout)* Follow that star.
Davina	... And he's the star...
All	*(Chant)* He's a star, he's a star, shine, shine!
Davina	...The shepherds are gone...
Shepherds	*(Off-stage)* Baa.
Davina	The angels have fallen...
Angels	*(Off-stage and off-key)* Alleluia.
Davina	Mary and Joseph are out of the picture...
All	*(Gasp with horror)*
Davina	Then who are you?
Voice 3	Us?
Davina	Yes, you!
Voice 1	Well, we're, eh - we're, eh - we're... *(Has idea)* ...Gold!
Voice 2	Frank.
Voice 3	Incense.
Voice 5	And Myrrh!

Davina	Four *very* gifted people indeed. I'm afraid we're running out of time - participants, you have 20 seconds to impress.
Narrator	Remember, it's up to you, the audience, to vote. Who will leave the Wee Brother stable next? Will it be the star?
Star	*(Shout)* Shine, shine.
Narrator	Or the wise men?
Wise men	*(Point and shout)* Follow that star.
Narrator	Join us next week for the very last exciting episode of Wee Brother - from all of us, good bye!

PART FOUR

Narrator	Welcome to this, the final episode of Wee Brother. Find out who's been voted out and who has won - are the wise men wise enough?
Wise men	*(Point and shout)* Follow that star.
Narrator	Is the star bright enough?
Star	*(Shout)* Shine, shine.
Davina	Wee Brother stable, this is Davina.
All	*('Hi', 'hello', shuffle etc.)*
Davina	The results of this, the final straw poll, are as follows...

W. Man 1   Hey, wait a minute…

             Davina looks shocked, the others in the stable try to shush him.

             No I won't be quiet. How can wise men like us be so daft?

W. Man 2   It's okay, it's…

All   'Only a game show, only a game show.'

W. Man 1   No it's not! This is supposed to be a nativity play.

W. Man 3   …and your problem is?

W. Man 1   Well, what's a nativity play?

W. Man 2   It's about a baby born in a stable.

Mary/Jo   *(Come in, stand holding baby) And* the young couple who cared for him.

Shepherd 1   It's about shepherds hearing angels…

Angels   *(Sing)* Alleluia …Angels who sang 'Glory to God in the highest…' … 'And on earth peace and goodwill to all.'

Shepherd 1   Yeah, exactly!

Shepherd 2   And they told us to go and see the baby for ourselves.

Shepherd 3   So we did. We saw him.

Shepherd 1   And we went home *soooo* happy!

W. Man 1   We're in the story too. We follow a special star.

Wise men	(Point and shout) Follow that star.
Star	(Shout) Shine, shine.
W. Man 2	And it's the star of course, who takes us to where the baby is sleeping.
W. Man 3	Not in a palace as we might have expected, but in a stable.
W. Man 1	In beside the animals, on some hay. We took our gifts in...
1/Gold	Gold. (Waving)
2/Frank	Frank. (Waving)
3/Incense	Incense. (Waving)
5/Myrrh	And Myrrh. (Waving)
W. Man 2	And we knew straightaway he was the one we'd been looking for...

Moment of silence as if lost in thought...

W. Man 1	If we throw out the shepherds and the angels and Mary and Joseph and either the wise men or the star, then we're really throwing the baby out with the bath water.
Star	Oh that is so cruel!

Everyone turns to look at him in disbelief.

What? What did I say?

Shepherd 1	It's just a figure of speech - you're not supposed to take it literally.
Star	I knew that! (Timidly) Shine, shine?

W. Man 1	If we throw everyone out, then there won't be any story left.
W. Man 2	No special birth to celebrate.
W. Man 1	No one to give presents to…

Everyone looks shocked as the thought of no Christmas dawns on them.

Davina	Wee Brother stable, this is Davina. The results of this week's straw poll are as follows…

Everyone sticks fingers in ears - Davina mouths silently, then disappears. Narrator begins to sing first verse of 'Once in Royal David's city, girls verse 2, boys verse 3, everyone else remaining verses.

Star	So who won? Was it me? (Shouts) Shine, shine!

Everyone groans.

Joseph	Star my boy, let me explain something to you - with Christmas, everyone's a winner.

Leads him away.

Narrator	There we must leave the Wee Brother stable - *full* instead of empty - but always with room for more. Happy Christmas!

When Bethlehem hit Bedrock!

Characters:

Narrator
Fred
Wilma
Barney
Betty
Angel
Shepherd 1
Shepherd 2
Shepherd 3
Star
Wise Man 1
Wise Man 2
Wise Man 3
Mr Slate/Innkeeper

Sound effects:

Radio 'theme tune' music
Dinosaur noise
Cymbal clash or drum roll
Thunderclap

PART ONE

Narrator	What if…? What if the Flintstones were asked to tell the Christmas story? How would Fred and Wilma, Barney and Betty, fare?
Fred	(*Comes running in*) Yabbadabbadoo!
Wilma	(*Walking in*) Fred? Is that you? Why all the excitement?

Fred	Wilma, Christmas is just around the corner!
Wilma	Fred, are you all right? You don't normally start thinking about Christmas until the shops are closed... it's only the 1st of December - 23 more shopping days to go!
Fred	Wilma, it's such an exciting time...
Wilma	Are you running a temperature, Fred? Come and sit down and I'll call Dino to come and lick you till you're cool...
Fred	I don't *want* to be licked. I don't *need* cooling down. You and me Wilma, we're going to have a baby!
Wilma	Fred are you sure you're all right? Just sit there, I'm going to fetch Barney and Betty.
Fred	It's okay, they know all about it.
Wilma	They do?
Fred	... and they're just as excited as I am.
Wilma	They are?
	Enter Barney and Betty.
Barney	Hiya, Fred
Betty	Hi Wilma! Hi, Fred!
Barney	Wilma, Fred told us your wonderful news - that's great!
Wilma	It is?
Betty	It's so exciting!

Barney	And it's so nice of you to let us have a part in it all.
Betty	(Grabbing Wilma's arm) Well that's what friends are for, Barney - sharing life's more precious moments...
Wilma	Betty, you and I need to talk...
Betty	Sure Wilma - Mom!!!
	The two women exit.
Barney	Wilma doesn't seem to be as excited as I though she'd be, Fred - is something wrong? I thought she'd be a lot more upbeat - what exactly did you say to her?
Fred	I told her what was happening - that Christmas is coming...
Barney	You told her you two are Mary and Joseph in Bedrock Radio's Nativity Play...
Fred	Yeah, of course I told her.
Barney	Funny, I thought she'd have been really pleased.
Fred	Well, I sorta told her.
Barney	What do you mean you sorta told her? Think back Fred, what exactly did you say?
Fred	I came in from work- I shouted 'Yabbadabbadoo' as you do when you're excited - then I told her Christmas is coming and we're going to have a baby!
Barney	Aaaah.
Fred	Aaaah, what Barney?

Barney	Fred, you didn't mention Mary and Joseph are the parents of the baby she's going to have...
Fred	How else is she going to get a baby by Christmas?

Girls return, Betty mopping Wilma's brow.

Wilma	I am so relieved Betty, I thought Fred had really flipped this time...
Betty	The only trouble with doing a nativity play round here, Wilma, is going to be finding 3 wise *men*...
Barney	Hey, Fred! If you're Joseph and Wilma's Mary... what about Betty and me - who are we gonna be?
Fred	Wait and see, Barney, wait and see
Narrator	Will Fred and Wilma get the Christmas message? How will they make use of Barney and Betty? Will there be a part for Dino? Come back next week to hear more of...When Bethlehem Hit Bedrock!

PART TWO

Narrator	What if...? What if the Flintstones were asked to tell the Christmas story? Last week Fred broke the news to Wilma that they were going to be Mary and Joseph in Bedrock Radio's Nativity Play - join us now for episode two of...'When Bethlehem hit Bedrock!'

Fred and Barney are standing at microphones with headphones on - sound effects in wings.

Fred	(Over rippling tune theme, gradually fading out) Once upon a time...

Barney	You can't start like that, Fred, this isn't a made up story, this is for real.
Fred	I suppose you're right, Barney - how about; one day, long, long ago an angel appeared to a young woman…
Barney	Fred - you can't say that.
Fred	What do you mean I can't say that, I just did!
Barney	I know you did, Fred, but you're Joseph - you need someone else to tell the story so that you can come in as Joseph.
Fred	I do? But who…?
Betty	Well, it can't be Wilma, because she's Mary but it needs someone with authority and intelligence and wit that can hold the whole play together…
	Pause.
	Do you think Dino's up to it?
	Dinosaur noise.
Fred	Or Barney! Barney could do it, couldn't you, Barney boy?
Barney	Gee, I dunno, Fred…
Fred	Sure you can, Barney! Go on, give it a go!
Barney	Oh, okay, Fred. Here goes. *(Cymbal clash - or drum roll)* One day, long, long ago an angel appeared to a young woman.
Fred	That's excellent, Barney.

Barney	Thanks Fred. The angel said…
Angel	(Entering quietly) Peace be with you! The Lord is with you and has greatly blessed you!
Barney	Fred, this is quite exciting isn't it?
Fred	It certainly is, Barney, it certainly is.
Angel	(Coughs to get attention) Don't be afraid, Mary; God has been gracious to you. You will become pregnant and give birth to a son, and you will name him Jesus…
Barney	The young woman was called Mary and she was promised to Joseph in marriage… Fred, do you think Joseph believed her when she told him what was going to happen?
Fred	I don't think so, Barney. He wanted to divorce her, remember, but he had a visit from an angel too…
Angel	(A bit annoyed) Yes - and I told him not to be afraid to take Mary as his wife - so he did.
Fred	Barney, are all angels as touchy?
Barney	I dunno, Fred, I haven't met many…
Wilma	(Stage whisper) The story, boys - back to the story.
Barney	Oh, yeah! Then Joseph and Mary set out on a journey.
Fred	(Reading badly) We had to go to Bethlehem to register because that is where my family came from.
Barney	You did that well, Fred.

Fred	Thank you, Barney - but I am a professional after all...
Barney	Meanwhile there were, out in the fields, some shepherds tending their sheep *(Lots of baa noises from off-stage)*
Shepherd 1	Look there's a sheep. *(Baa)*
Shepherd 2	And there's one. *(Baa)*
Shepherd 3	And there's another. *(Baa)*
Shepherd 1	Let's tend them.
Barney	When all of a sudden there was a great light in the sky... *(Thunderclap)* ...and the sound of singing... *(Off-stage singing from rest of cast)* The Shepherds were petrified. *(Sound of knocking)*
Fred	What's that supposed to be?
Barney	That's their knees knocking. Then an angel appeared.
Fred	Not the same one, I hope!
Angel	*(Through gritted teeth)* Do not be afraid!
Barney	The angel said.
Angel	I bring you news of great joy for all people. A baby has been born - he is Christ the Lord.
Barney	Exciting stuff - eh, Fred?
Angel	*(Annoyed again)* And this will be a sign to you - you will find a baby wrapped in cloths and lying in a manger.
Fred	Does the angel go now?

Barney	*(Turning over pages of script)* I think so, Fred…
Narrator	And so must we - there we leave it for another week - join us again, same time, same place next week for the next instalment of… When Bethlehem hit Bedrock!

PART THREE

Narrator	*What if…?* What if the Flintstones were asked to tell the Christmas story? Two weeks ago Fred broke the news to Wilma that they were going to be Mary and Joseph in Bedrock Radio's Nativity Play - last week the recording began and Fred and Barney met their match, in an angel with attitude. Let's see what this week brings in…'When Bethlehem hit Bedrock!'
Barney	Duhh! Where were we, Fred?
Fred	Standing around here, Barney.
Barney	No, in the story, Fred - where were we in the story?
Fred	Let me see…
Angel	I told Joseph he should take Mary as his wife.
Fred	Yeah, that's right! She told Joseph he should take Mary as his wife… and then… eh…
Angel	*Then,* despite being interrupted…
Barney	Did we interrupt the angel, Fred?
Fred	I think we might have done…

Angel	(*Threatening*) *Despite* being interrupted, I went on to tell the shepherds that a baby had been born and they were to make their way to Bethlehem where they would find him.
Fred	And then you, Barney, asked me if that's the last we'd see of the angel.
Barney	I did, Fred, I did...
	Pause.
	And is it?
Angel	You can't keep a good angel down! (*Disappears*)
Barney	I guess we'll just need to watch this space...
Wilma	Boys, do you think we could get on with the story - Betty and Dino are desperate to play their parts...
Barney	Of course, Wilma - and may I say how beautiful you look today with those precious rocks strung around your neck.
Wilma	Why thank you Barney, I bought them just last....
Barney	(*Interrupting*) Sorry Wilma - the show must go on. And behold a star appeared in the sky...
Star	(*Popping out of nowhere*) Shine, shine!
	Everyone cheers, star disappears.
Barney	...its route across the heavens tracked by wise star-gazers from the East.

Fred   How wise is it to stay up all night looking at stars?

Barney   I dunno, Fred - but that's what it says.

Betty   *(Overacting completely as Wise Man 1)* We saw the star...

Star   *(Popping up again)* Shine, shine.

            Everyone cheers, star disappears.

Betty   And knew straightaway it was special.

Fred   Barney, did he just sound like Betty?

Barney   I hope you're not suggesting my wife is manly!

Betty   *(Whispering)* Psst!... It *is* me - it's Betty - there just aren't too
            many women's parts in this story. *(Loud stage voice again)*
            So we followed the star.

Star   *(Popping up again)* Shine, shine.

            Everyone cheers, star disappears.

W. Man 2   We set off on camel back.

W. Man 3   And travelled for weeks.

W. Man 2   For months.

W. Man 3   Never losing sight of the star...

Star   *(Popping up again)* Shine, shine.

            Everyone cheers, star disappears.

W. Man 3   ...even for a moment.

Betty	Until it came to rest over a stable in Bethlehem.
Barney	You know, Fred, it's pretty amazing. All those stars up in the sky - hundreds of thousands of them! Millions! And these guys from the East, apart from one who sounded suspiciously like a girl, managed to spot the one special star that was to take them to Bethlehem... it makes you think...
Fred	It certainly does, Barney, it certainly does - don't they have anything better to do with their time?
Wilma	Fred, Barney's right. It's wonderful how they saw that star and pursued it.
Barney	And not an angel in sight.
Angel	Watch it, bro! I'm still here.
Narrator	It sounds like a good place to leave things for this week. The Shepherds have heard... The wise men have heard... Join us next week ... 'When Bethlehem Hit Bedrock!'

PART FOUR

Narrator	*What if...?* What if the Flintstones were asked to tell the Christmas story? So far we've met the shepherds and the wise men in the Bedrock Radio version of a Nativity Play - and an angel with attitude - join us now for the final episode of...'When Bethlehem hit Bedrock!'
Barney	This is your big moment, Wilma. We're coming to the bit in the stable.
Wilma	What do I have to say, Barney? Have I got many lines?
Barney	*(Looks down script)* Nope!

Wilma	But I thought you said it was my big moment?!
Barney	It is - but you just act excited.
Wilma	But this is radio, Barney - no one can *see* anything I do!
Barney	*(Shrugs)* You're the strong *silent* type.
Wilma	It doesn't seem right that I should carry the baby and have all the pain of childbirth and have nothing to say...
Barney	You're a ponderer.
Wilma	I'm nothing of the sort! If anything I'm Church of Scotland[1]!
Barney	No, Wilma. I mean you watch what's going on and 'ponder these things in your heart'.
Wilma	Who says?
Barney	The Good Book.
Wilma	It still doesn't seem fair...
Fred	*(Coming in)* Sorry I'm late, I was checking the availability of rooms at the Bethlehem Travel Lodge.
Wilma	And?
Fred	And they're fully booked. Not a bed to be had within a fifty-mile radius.
Barney	Which takes us neatly back to the story in hand. Mary and Joseph... *(Nudging Fred and Wilma, whispers)* That's you two... *(Loud again)* Mary and Joseph eventually arrived in their hometown of Bethlehem where, if you remember, they had to go to register. Mary's time to have her baby was very near but everywhere they went to find a bed was full.

1 Or substitute any other denomination that suits!

41

Fred	*(Reading badly)* Oh Mary, what are we going to do? No one will give us a room.
Barney	At every reception desk the same thing happened. The hoteliers shook their head and shrugged their shoulders - 'We're sorry,' they said, 'There's just no room.'

Pause.

	Hey Fred, can I have a word with you?
Fred	Sure, Barney, what is it?
Barney	Look Fred, I know what happens next and we need an innkeeper - who's going to do it?
Fred	Don't worry, Barney, it's all taken care of - we have a guest appearance from someone local[2].
Barney	A local figure... who's that Fred?
Fred	I'll fetch him. Just go on with the story...

Goes off-stage to get Mr Slate/the Innkeeper and bring him out.

Barney	The very last place they tried looked as busy as everywhere else but Fred - I mean- Joseph went in anyway. *(Whispering)* You ready, Fred?
Fred	Just about - keep going!
Barney	He asked the innkeeper if he had anywhere, anywhere at all they might lay their head. The innkeeper said...
Innkeeper	*(Entering)* I have no rooms left but I suppose you could use the stable. At least the hay is warm and clean.

2 We were fortunate to be able to use our local MP for this role -hence the applause! Though not essential, if you can come up with a local 'worthy' in act as Fred's 'Boss', it adds something to the occasion

Everyone applaud.

Barney | It's Mr. Slate the Quarry owner! - any chance of a pay rise, Sir?

Innkeeper | None.

Fred | So much for the season of goodwill...!

Barney | Mary and Joseph went into the stable and there the baby was born amid the sheep *(Baa-ing off-stage)* and the cattle *(Moo-ing)* and... Dino what are you doing there?! *(Dinosaur noises)* They were joined by the shepherds and the wise men who brought gifts for the child of ...

Betty | Gold.

W. Man 2 | Frankincense.

W. Man 3 | And myrrh.

Barney | They worshipped the child and went home rejoicing because they knew that what they had seen was special...

Pause.

Fred, that's a beautiful story.

Wilma | *(Quietly)* And the best part of all is that it doesn't end there.

Angel | The Good News is for everyone. God has come among us and he's here to stay. Peace be with you all!

Everyone | Happy Christmas!

Narrator | There we must leave the citizens of Bedrock. They've discovered God is with them. He's with us too. Love came down at Christmas... and stayed. Hallelujah!

Animal Stable

Characters:

Rolf Harris[1]
Innkeeper
Donkey
Joseph
Mary
Sheep 1
Sheep 2
Sheep 3
Camel 1
Camel 2
Camel 3
Star

Sound effects:

Recordings of 'Two little boys', 'Tie me Kangaroo Down Sport', or 'Animal Hospital Theme'
Love came down at Christmas (optional)

PART ONE

Scene: *A stable: a few bales of hay, pitchfork, etc. Mary and Joseph to front, Donkey in background.*

Music: *Animal Hospital theme, or 'Two little boys'.*

Rolf Harris   *(Shaking a wobbly board)* Welcome to the Christmas series of Animal Stable! We'll be here in the little town of Bethlehem for the next four weeks, catching up with some of the pets that pass through. Let me introduce you to our host and owner of this fine establishment who's raring to go - Al Fayed Up!

1 Rolf can be Rolf, or Rolfina, depending on who is available in your group; in the original performance, this part was taken by a woman - yes, with a beard!

44

Innkeeper	*(Seems really bored... walks in muttering)* Come at the busiest time of year, why don't you... Take the place over, turn good paying customers out... *(Sees people - instant smiles and gracious manner)* Ahh... hello there!... welcome to my humble abode!
Rolf Harris	Do you want to introduce us to anyone in particular?
Innkeeper	*(Aside again)* Yeah, my mother-in-law - that'll scare you! *(Aloud)* Come this way. We have a new arrival you should meet. A *Beasticus burdenus.*
Rolf Harris	A *Beasticus burdenus?*
Innkeeper	That's its Sunday name...
Rolf Harris	You mean an ass!
Donkey	I prefer the term donkey, myself.

Rolf Harris and Innkeeper react, startled, and run away in fright.

Ass has such negative vibes!

Joseph	Donkey! You should warn people you can speak.
Donkey	How can I do that without speaking? Sign language?

Sarcastically tries miming, 'I can speak.'

Joseph	Okay, okay, just as scary - point taken! We'd better see if those two are all right.
Rolf Harris	*(Creeping back)* We're fine, we're fine, honestly.

Looks round for Innkeeper, nowhere to be seen... shrugs.

Got the old heart going a bit, but we're fine - at least, I'm fine.

Donkey	You want to ask me how I am, then?
Rolf Harris	I'm not sure I've ever interviewed a donkey before...
Donkey	I've come from a town called Nazareth - with these two and a half.
Rolf	Two and a half...?
Donkey	Mary has a 'bump' - a baby on the way.
Mary	It's due very soon, but we had to come here to register.
Rolf Harris	*(Laughing)* Not *too* soon, I hope... where's the nearest maternity unit?
Joseph	You're standing on it.
	Rolf looks down and lifts feet in shock.
Donkey	Hey! This is an *animal* programme... You're supposed to be interested in *me, moi!* The most famous donkey in all history!
Rolf Harris	There aren't too many historical donkeys... hysterical maybe...
	Donkey looks hurt.
Mary	*(Stroking Donkey)* Donkey, you're not just the most famous, you're the most important donkey in all history.
Donkey	I am? Hey, I am! *(Looking smug)*
Mary	Wait and see! You've carried someone very special - very special indeed.
Donkey	Who, Mary? Who?

| Mary | Wait and see! |

| Rolf Harris | I'm afraid we're running out of time. Tune in again next week and we'll see how Donkey recovers from his long journey, and meet a few of the other residents of the Animal Stable. |

Music: *'Animal Hospital' theme, or 'Tie me Kangaroo down, Sport'.*

PART TWO

Theme Music: *Animal Hospital or 'Two little boys'.*

| Rolf Harris | Rolf Harris with you again. Good you could join us, here in the Animal Stable! Last week we met up with a donkey who'd just arrived in town. He came with a young couple and the young lady was about to have a baby. We're going to follow that story up and see how she's doing. |

| Donkey | I'm doing fine, thank you! I'm all rested up. Had some nice fresh hay, feel on top… |

| Rolf Harris | Actually, Donkey, I was thinking more of Mary… |

| Donkey | Mary?! |

Goes off in a huff to side of stage.

| Mary | *(Looking into crib)* I'm doing fine too, thank you. |

| Rolf Harris | Awww, has the little fella arrived, then? Safe and sound? |

| Mary | Safe and sound! |

| Rolf Harris | *(Sings softly)* Tie me Kangaroo down, Sport, tie me… |

Donkey	(*From side stage*) Well, I hope everyone is enjoying this *animal* programme, where the *animals* are being ignored... (*Muttering*) So much for the *animals*...

Whistling and cries of 'Come by!' from off stage.

What's that?

The three Sheep are 'herded' in by the Innkeeper.

Innkeeper	Sorry to disturb you people just now - but can we squeeze a few sheep in?
Donkey	With or without mint sauce?

Everyone turns to look at Donkey who shrugs.

What? What have I said?

Innkeeper	These guys came down off the hills for some reason. They'll need to stay somewhere - so why not here - the rates are reasonable... come on in you three.
Sheep 1	Thank heeeh-vens, we're heeehre at laaaah-st.

Innkeeper stares - scratches head, mouth open, gets more amazed as conversation goes on.

Sheep 2	Beeeeh-tter late than neeeh-ver.
Sheep 3	(*Posh voice*) Oh, *do* stop bleating, the two of you. You didn't *have* to come you know... You could easily have stayed behind.
Sheep 1	'Aaaa-ll we like sheep', as they say... we're in this together Baa-arney, and Baa-arbara.

Sheep 3	We have not gone astray. We were told to come here.
Sheep 2	We were told to come...? Us? Ewe sure?
Sheep 3	(Defensively) The heavenly host weren't looking anywhere in particular when they said, 'Don't be afraid' - in fact I'm sure they said they had 'good news for ewes...' They could only have meant us.
Rolf Harris	Hold on a minute - do all the animals in this place speak?
Donkey	Man, you're fast. He's fast, isn't he?
Innkeeper	(Wandering off) Maybe I should bottle some of the water round here... sell it... Bethlehem Babble, it's got a nice ring to it...
Rolf Harris	So have you come here to lamb?...
Donkey	(Quietly) Mint sauce...
Rolf Harris	(Ignoring Donkey) ...or just for some rest and relaxation?
Sheep 2	He-ey, ba-aby!
Rolf Harris	Oh for food! Of course, for hay!
Sheep 1	No, just ba-aby.
Rolf Harris	I'm sorry, you've lost me - you're here to lamb then, right enough?
Sheep 3	No we've come to see the baby. At least, I have.
Sheep 1	We aaaall have.
Rolf Harris	Mary's baby? I know he's lovely, but...

Joseph	Mary *and* Joseph's baby. He takes his good looks from his father.
Mary	Yes, they're heavenly.
Donkey	*(Coming back to the centre)* In fact, just divine!
	Innkeeper returns with a big bottle of water.
Rolf Harris	Hold on - how did you three sheep stuck up on the hills come to know about this baby here?
Sheep 3	I told you, the heavenly host. *They* said, 'Today in the town of David, a Saviour has been born to you; he is Christ the Lord. This will be a sign to you: you will find a baby wrapped in cloths and lying in a manger.' So we've come. Looking for the baby.
Innkeeper	*(Checks bottle and takes a big swig)* Talking donkeys, talking sheep, special babies - man, this stuff's good!
Rolf Harris	Much as I know you'd love to stay with us - we have to go now. We'll catch up with the Donkey and the sheep next week and no doubt we'll meet some more interesting characters. Till then…
	Music: 'Animal Hospital', or 'Tie me Kangaroo down, Sport'.

⬻────◯✕◯────⬺

PART THREE

Scene: *Stable with Mary and Joseph, sheep and Donkey. Innkeeper hanging about. Star hidden in pulpit².*

Music: *'Animal Hospital' theme, or 'Two little boys'.*

---

2 Or somewhere else suitable in your location, where he can be concealed.

Rolf Harris	Good you could join us again here in the Animal Stable. We've met some amazing pets in the last couple of weeks and something tells me we're going to meet some more today. You'll be pleased to hear that Donkey is still with us.
Donkey	*(Waving frantically and shouting)* That's me, that's me!
Rolf Harris	And the sheep are still here too...
All sheep	*(Standing and taking a bow)* Buuuuht of course!
Rolf Harris	And of course we have Mary and Joseph and little Junior...
Donkey	Jesus - His name's *Jesus* - don't you do *any* research for this programme...? But let's get back to the *animals*. *(Looking pathetic)* Now that you ask, I'm feeling soooo much better now that I'm all rested up - although the hay could do with being changed a little more often and the place is getting a little too crowded for such a sensitive animal as me...
Innkeeper	*(Comes into stable, looking off to the side)* Just come this way, your Kingships. The camels can stay here - there's *plenty* of room for them.
	Enter camels. Innkeeper shepherds them into the stable.
Rolf Harris	Is that *more* business for your stable?
Innkeeper	It certainly is - but I think this lot will be quieter than her/him. *(Points to Donkey)*
Donkey	Me? Noisy? Me? I've a good mind to take the hump! *(Nose in air...)*
Innkeeper	Well, we've got three here you could perhaps take with you - space is kind of limited.

Sheep 2	Meeeeh-be we should go outside.
Donkey	Yeah, you do that ewe three sheep, and we'll all have some more elbow-room.
	Sheep make to go.
Joseph	*(In a warning voice)* Donkey...
Donkey	*(Looking sheepishly guilty)* What? They suggested it - I'm only agreeing with them.
Joseph	Sheep, don't go. You've come a long way to see our son and you need your rest now. Stay. It might be a bit cramped, but there's room for all of us - *(Turning to Donkey)* isn't there, Donkey...?
Donkey	*(With a fixed smile)* Of course there is... *(Sniffs the air)* What's that fishy smell?
	Everyone sniffs.
Donkey	Oh silly me, it's because we're all like sardines in here...
Rolf Harris	Camels, can I ask what brings you here?
Innkeeper	Oh don't tell me, *they* speak too!
	Sits down on hay holding head in hands.
Camel 1	We've come a long way.
Camel 2	To see him.
Camel 3	With heavy loads.
Donkey	Yeah, those kings were pretty big, I noticed that...

Rolf Harris	Did you hear a heavenly choir telling you to come here - just as the sheep did?
Camel 1	No, we didn't *hear* anything.
Camel 2	We followed what we *saw*.
Camel 3	And what we saw... was a star.
Donkey	Well, I wouldn't go that far, this is my third TV appearance, but I'm hardly a star... More a tiny meteor, but I'm hoping for bigger things...
Joseph	*(Warning voice)* Donkey...
Donkey	What? What did I say this time?
Camel 1	We followed a star from the East.
Donkey	Oh, I see, someone like Bruce Lee in Kung Fu fighting...
Camel 2	A bright star. Brighter than any other.
Camel 3	And we followed it here.
Donkey	Bruce Lee is here? In Bethlehem? Ayeee ha!
	Does a pretend karate chop.
Camel 1	That star.
	Points to where Star is hidden. Everyone except Donkey looks. Star pops up and raises arms.
Star	Shine, shine!
	Everyone cheers, Star disappears.

Donkey	What star?
Camel 2	*That star (Points again to Star's hiding-place)*
	Everyone looks, including Donkey, Star pops up.
Star	Shine, shine!
	Everyone cheers, Star disappears again.
Donkey	Ohhh! *That* star.
Star	*(Popping up again)* Shine, shine!
	Everyone cheers, Star disappears again.
Donkey	Does he do that every time we say...
Joseph	*(Warning)* Donkey!
Camel 3	It tells us that here a new King is born.
Innkeeper	Talking donkeys, talking sheep, talking camels... now talking stars. Retirement sounds good.
Donkey	*(Goes to comfort Innkeeper)* Oh, now don't you let all this get you down - especially not *that star.*
Star	*(Popping up again)* Shine, shine.
	Everyone cheers, Star disappears again.
Joseph	*(Warning)* Donkey!
Rolf Harris	Perhaps this would be a good time to leave the Animal Stable... We have one more visit to make before the end of the series - be sure and join us - find out more about 'that star...'

Star	*(Popping up again)* Shine, shine.

Everyone cheers, star disappears again.

Rolf Harris	...Donkey, the sheep and the camels, Mary and Joseph and the little fella. See you next week, then, bye!

Music: *'Animal Hospital'*, or *'Tie me Kangaroo down, Sport.'*

PART FOUR

Scene: *Donkey, sheep, camels, Mary and Joseph are all in the stable. Rolf Harris out front. The innkeeper has a big suitcase. Star hidden again in pulpit or other hiding place.*

Music: *'Animal Hospital' Theme or 'Two little boys'.*

Rolf Harris	So this is it. Our very last visit to the Animal Stable. I should let you know that there is now a website where you can chat to Donkey; it's at www.assonline. The sheep are still here and are well rested - as are the camels - and all under the care of the energetic, if somewhat mystified, Al Fayed Up, the local innkeeper and owner of these stables.
Innkeeper	Not for much longer.
Rolf Harris	I'm sorry?
Innkeeper	Not for much longer. I'm getting out. It was bad enough when that donkey arrived but it got worse when the sheep came and even worse still when those kingly camels happened by... but the star, the star took the biscuit.
Rolf Harris	What star?
Innkeeper	*Please* don't make me say it.

Donkey	Okay then, I'll say it - *that* star.
Star	*(Popping up again, waving vigorously)* Shine, shine!
	Everyone cheers, Star disappears again.
Donkey	Boy, do I enjoy doing that. It's the most animated I've ever seen him, will I do it again...?
Joseph	*(Warning voice)* Donkey...!
Innkeeper	I don't think life will ever be the same again after this census.
Joseph	It won't be the same for any of us.
Donkey	No indeedy, Joseph, from here on in you and Mary are going to be up all night, changing nappies!
Sheep 1	We'll be heaaaading off soon too.
	Sheep make a move to leave.
Sheep 2	I don't think we'll ever forgeeeht this place.
Donkey	I know what you mean. The brochure said it was an open plan room, full of rustic charm, but this isn't quite what I imagined...
Sheep 3	I don't think we'll ever forget *who* we met here.
Camel 1	Neither will we. *(Getting up to go)*
Camel 2	As we carry our Kings.
Camel 3	And head back East.
Camel 1	Our thoughts will always come back to the very special person we shared our quarters with.

Donkey	Oh gee guys. I'm touched. That is *sooo* nice of you. I'll never forget you, either.
Sheep 3	We're not talking about you.
Donkey	Rolf, then. You'll remember Rolf.
Camel 1	We're not talking about him either.
Camel 3	Although it's been a definite pleasure meeting him. *(Snuggling up to Rolf)*
Innkeeper	I don't know - someone who sings about tying kangaroos down while fronting an animal programme, it doesn't seem quite right, does it...
Camel 2	We're talking about the baby.
Donkey	The baby. Of course! I knew that. You'll always remember this place because of the baby....
	Pause.
	Why?
Joseph	Donkey, remember we said you'd carried someone special here? Someone very special? This is that very special person.
	Mary carries the baby forward.
	We don't know yet what's in store for him but we know it's something big, something important, something no one else can do.
Sheep 1	Which is why the angels told us...
Sheep 2	Aaaand our shepherds.

Sheep 3	To come down off the hills to this stable.
Camel 1	It's why we came here from the East.
Camel 2	In search of a king.
Camel 3	By the light of that star.
	Points to Star's hiding-place, Star pops up again.
Star	*(Quietly)* Shine, shine.
All	Ahhhhh.
	Star disappears again.
Donkey	Mary, a penny for your thoughts.
Mary	I'll remember this time in the stable… with *all* of you. Even you, Donkey. My guess is we've all played a part in a very important story - one which has only just begun…
Rolf Harris	This may be our last visit to the Animal Stable, but I suspect it's not going to be the last we hear of many of the people we've met here. Look out for Donkey in years to come when he carries Jesus once more - reprising his first important role. But far more importantly, watch the baby grow up and see if he really is as special as all of us here in the Animal Stable, seem to think. Thank you for joining us… and bye for now.

Music *(suggested:) Love came down at Christmas.*

Jesus Christ and the Stable of Promise

Characters:

Narrator
Mary
Joseph
Professors 1& 2 (male)
Professor 3 (female)
Shepherds 1,2 & 3
Angels (at least two)
Innkeeper

PART ONE

Narrator   A long time ago in the very real world, a promise was made that a very special child would be born. That child would have very ordinary parents who would care for him and watch over him as he grew. He would have no extraordinary powers to help him through life. People would see him as one of them until, when the time was right he would show the world, not his great power, but his great courage... Then looking back they would turn to his birth and see there, Jesus Christ and the Stable of Promise...

Enter two men and a woman wearing academic gowns armed with telescopes, binoculars, a map etc.

Professor 1   Well, Professor, what do you think?

Professor 2   I think we're on to something, Professor. Something big.

Opens up a map and studies it although the map is upside down.

Professor 3   Something important.

Professor 1   My feelings exactly! This is the moment we've been waiting for. Working for. This is why we've studied and spent all these years honing and fine-tuning our star-gazing skills. These are serious matters we are about - calling on all we've learned. I sense the moment of truth is very near. This is where all roads have been leading, where all paths should meet, all routes end...

Professor 2   *(Looking up from map)* What? Here in Dornoch[1]?

Professor 3   Professor, I worry about you. *(Turns his map up the right way)* I think we should leave. Now.

Professor 1   Straight away!

Professor 3   Without delay!

              1 and 3 start getting ready to go.

Professor 2   Do you not think it would be better to wait till morning? It's a bit dark just now and it'll be easier to see where we're going if we wait till morning...

              Professor 1 and 3 stop dead and look at each other, askance..

Professor 3   Professor, what are we?

Professor 2   Well, I'm tall, dark and handsome, he's short, fair and...

Professor 3   *(Interrupting)* We're astronomers! Astronomers!

Professor 1   *Star-gazers.*

Professor 3   And when do stars come out?

Professor 1   Actually, they don't 'come out' at all. That's a misnomer. They're there all the time - it's just that...

1 Or use appropriate local town/suburb name.

Professor 3   (*Totally ignoring Professor 1*) At *night*. When it's *dark*. *That's* when we can see the stars - and we need to be able to see them before we can follow them. Night-time. We need to go NOW!

She bustles off the stage and down the aisle, gown flapping.

Professor 1   Now see what you've done! She always scares me when she goes off in a rage like that - she'll get on that camel and strike out for Bethlehem!

Professor 2   You mean she'll go really fast?

Professor 1   No - she'll just keep striking things - us included…

Professor 2   (*Shouts after Professor 3*) Professor!

Professor 3   (*From back of audience*) Now what?

Professor 2   (*Pointing in opposite direction*) It's this way (*Nudges and whispers to Professor 1*) Just like a woman to go off at a tangent! (*Loud again*) It's this way.

Professor 1   (*Shaking head*) I have a feeling this is going to be the most trying of times for us all…

Professor 2   In more ways than one!

Professor 3   (*Back with the other Professors*) Have we got everything we need?

Professor 1   Food, gifts, our great knowledge and wealth…

Professor 2   Boo!

Professor 1   (*Jumps*) What was that for?

Professor 2   (With a mock Chinese accent) Supplies! Supplies! (Both look blankly at him as he tries to explain) Supplies - food, water, the presents - this is going to be a long, long journey...

Professor 3   Then it's time we were off. (Professor 2 makes a show of holding his nose) What's wrong with you now?

Professor 2   I was wondering what the strange smell was... we're off - geddit...?!

               Professors 3 and 1 groan, pile everything on Professor 2 and walk off.

Professor 3   See! That's what comes of going to Edinburgh University[2]...

               Professor 2 follows the others...

Narrator   A star whose brightness none has seen before. Leading these learned people to what? To where? To whom? Join us again soon for the climax to this magical but true tale of Jesus Christ and the Stable of Promise.

PART TWO

Narrator   To what? To where? To whom? It sounds like an owl but not an owl in sight... Where are our three wise Professors being led? What great and marvellous discovery awaits them...? As they set off on their journey to follow the star, in another place a very ordinary couple are beginning to experience very extraordinary things... the coming together of two very different worlds. Join us now for this next episode in the tale of Jesus Christ and the Stable of Promise...

Mary   Letter floats down from above her... she reads it.

               A letter! For me! From nowhere - what does it say...? 'Peace be with you! The Lord is with you and has greatly blessed you!' What's that all about?

2 Or use the most appropriate (or inappropriate!) institution's name

Another letter floats down.

Another one! This is worse than Hogwarts!.. But why to me? *(Reads)* 'Don't be afraid, Mary; God has been gracious to you. You will become pregnant and give birth to a son, and you will name him Jesus...'

Another letter floats down.

Another letter - where are they all coming from? What does this one say? 'He will be great' it says, 'and will be called Son of the Most High God. The Lord God will make him a king as his ancestor David was and he will be the king of the descendants of Jacob forever; his kingdom will never end! Is someone pulling my leg? Joseph! Joseph - where are you? Come here!

Joseph *(Coming in)* What is it, Mary?

Mary Look at all these - they just dropped down from nowhere - they say we're going to have a baby, *God's* baby - the same as us but very different from us. Joseph, a baby! You and me!

Joseph *(Looking up for letters - a bit worried)* You.... me? Now hang on a minute Mary, if my mum gets wind of this - if my *Gran* hears of it...

Another letter floats down.

Where did that come from?! *(Picks it up, looking up again)* Look Mary, don't take this personally, but who's going to believe it's not me who got you into this position? *(Opens letter)* Maybe we should split up... *(Reads letter aloud)* 'Joseph, don't be afraid to take Mary home as your wife because what is conceived in her is of the Holy Spirit. She will give birth to a son, and you will name him Jesus because he will save his people from their sins.' Spooky...

63

Looks up and around for more letters.

Mary   Joseph, this seems to be what *God* wants us to do...

Silence... no reaction from Joseph who's still looking up.

Joseph are you listening to me...? Joseph! Joseph!

She shakes him.

Joseph   What? Huh? Oh, I'm sorry, I was waiting for another letter - you got a few so I thought I might too... maybe telling me he'd have a special mark on his forehead or something so that *everyone* would know who he is...

Mary   Joseph, be serious - this isn't a story made up by a single mum in a coffee shop - it's reality - the truth! God wants us, you and me, to have his child!

Joseph   If that's right, Mary, then... do you want the good news or the bad news?

Mary   Give me the good news first.

Joseph   Well...

Mary   No, make it the bad and then maybe the good will soften the blow.

Joseph   Well...

Mary   No, the good, Joseph, give me the good - not the bad...

Joseph   Mary, give me a chance here! *I'll* choose. Let me get my head straight first though... you're going to have a baby - God's baby *(Looks up again)* - my Gran *might* just go for that... *(Thinks)* Okay Mary, I'll marry you!

| Mary | Is that the good news or the bad? |

| Joseph | You're pushing it... the *bad* news is that once you're my wife, you and I are going to have to go to Bethlehem in Judah. Everyone's been told that they have to go to their hometown for some big census and that's where my family comes from. |

| Mary | Bethlehem... |

| Joseph | And since broomsticks and magic cars are not an option, perhaps we should set out as soon as possible - get packing now, in fact - it might be sensible to put as much distance as we can between me and my Gran... until the dust settles, of course. |

Another floating letter comes down.

| Mary | *(Picks up the letter)* Another letter. *(Reading)* 'Bethlehem in the land of Judah, you are by no means least of the leading cities of Judah: for from you will come a leader who will guide my people Israel.' Joseph, let's go... |

Both exit.

| Narrator | Here ends the second chapter of Jesus Christ and the Stable of Promise. What adventures lie ahead for the young couple and their, as yet, unborn child? Will a hairy giant leave the baby at Mary and Joseph's door? Will the boy be given his own owl? Be given a bedroom under the stairs? Join us next week for the next exciting chapter of... Jesus Christ and the Stable of Promise... |

PART THREE

Narrator   Floating letters. Strange goings on. Promises and hints of promises. What adventures await us now? Is this truly the child of everyone's dreams? Let's turn again to the story of Jesus Christ and the Stable of Promise...

Mary and Joseph are en route to Bethlehem...

Joseph   What did your letter say again, Mary?

Mary   Which one? There were lots of them remember? They all came floating down from nowhere. As if they'd dropped from the claws of some passing bird.

Joseph   The one about giving birth to a son we're to call Jesus and his being of David's line - a king who will reign over his people for ever.

Mary   The one you've obviously learned off by heart?

Joseph   Well, it's not every day you get floating notes telling you you're going to be the parents of a special child.

Mary   Special *and* long-awaited.

Joseph   Yeah, nine months is quite a while.

Mary   No - this child's been due for centuries.

Joseph   Why does that thought give me goose-bumps?

Mary   Joseph, I think... *(Stops)*

Joseph   Are you OK, Mary? You're not in pain, are you?

Mary   Joseph, I think there's an awful lot more to this child than we'll ever know and somehow I think we're not the only ones expecting him.

Joseph	Of course others know! It took some explaining but my mum now knows he's coming - and my Gran. And your mum knows...
Mary	I mean more than just our families.
Joseph	You're right! If my Gran knows then half the village will too - she'll have told everyone! Even if it did take her a while to believe it's God who got you into this state and not me.

Mary shudders.

Joseph	You're not cold, Mary, are you?
Mary	It's just I'm remembering my sister's reaction. 'We'll not be having any of that religious mumbo jumbo in *our* family!' she said - and she meant it! I think she'd rather have had me hidden away under the stairs than let me come into contact with anyone else - can't she see the promise and hope this child offers us all?
Joseph	At the moment all I hope is that we can find somewhere to spend the night - Bethlehem is going to be packed!
Mary	He's expected, Joseph. He's expected.
Joseph	And so is the whole of the line of David... and Bethlehem only has the one Travel-lodge...

Exit Mary and Joseph, enter Shepherds 1, 2 & 3.

Shepherd 1	It's not fair. Everyone else counts sheep to help them get to sleep - we'd get the sack, not hit it, if *we* nodded off.
Shepherd 2	*(Counting)* Three hundred and sixty-seven, three hundred and sixty-eight, three hundred and -

Shepherd 3 - So what are we shepherds supposed to do when we want to sleep - eh? Tell me that!

Shepherd 2 That's easy - we just lie on the edge of our beds - we'll soon drop off! *(Losing count)* Aaaargh! One, two, three, four, five…

Shepherd 1 There should be a law against it.

Shepherd 3 What? Against counting sheep?

Shepherd 1 Well - at least a charter for shepherds defending our right to…

Shepherd 2 …thirty-four, thirty-five, thirty-six, to fall asleep on the job! Yeah, right! *(Loses count again)* Aaargh! One, two…

Shepherd 1 No other profession is referred to as a main-course dish…

Shepherd 3 My wife says Russell Crowe is quite a dish.

Shepherd 2 …Eleven, twelve, thirteen, mine prefers Ewan MacGregor - or even Sean Connery. *(Keeps counting)* Yes! Fourteen, fifteen, sixteen…

Shepherd 1 They don't have actors' sauce, or clerical stew. There's no such thing as doctors' flan or teachers' torte.

Shepherd 3 I thought *all* teachers torte?

Shepherd 2 *(Loses count again with a groan)* Aaaaaaaaargh! One, two, three, four…

Shepherd 1 *(Ignoring them both)* There's shepherd's pie, though - why should we be thought of as full of mince and half-baked?

Shepherd 3 We just have a poor image.

Shepherd 1 It's not just my image that's poor - look at that… *(Turns out pockets)* Not a bean to my name!

Shepherd 2   *Snores loudly.*

Shepherd 1   Oh no - he's sleeping! Now we're for it - the boss will send a screamer - wait for it!

The two shepherds put their hands over their ears and screw their eyes tight shut... an angelic chorus strikes up.Enter Angels, appearing on high, singing from the Hallelujah Chorus. Shepherds 1 and 3 stand with mouths open...

Angels   Hallelujah!

Shepherd 2   *(Wakes up)* I'm sorry! I didn't mean to - it won't happen again... wait a minute! That's too tuneful for a screamer...

Shepherd 1   It's... it's... it's...

Shepherd 3   Heavenly!

Shepherd 1   Divine!

Shepherd 2   It's certainly different!

Shepherd 3   Sssh! Listen to what they're saying.

Angel 1   Don't be afraid.

Angel 2   We're here with good news for you which will bring great joy to everyone.

Angel 1   Today in David's town your Saviour was born.

Angel 2   And this shall be your sign.

Shepherd 2   A baby! All together now, *awwwww!...*

Angel 2   *(Coughs and looks pointedly at Shepherd 2)* And this shall be your sign. You will find a baby wrapped in strips of cloth and lying in a manger.

Shepherd 1   Come on! Let's go!

Shepherd 2   Go? Go where?

Shepherd 3   To find the baby.

Shepherd 2   And leave the sheep? No way! Then we really would start hearing things! Back to counting. One, two, three, four...

Shepherd 1   Suit yourself!

Shepherds 1 and 3 run off.

Shepherd 2   ...ninety-nine, one hundred - wait for me! I'm coming too!

Runs after the others.

Narrator   No screamers - just an angelic choir. No magical pyrotechnics - just some shell-shocked shepherds... Join us next week to hear more in the fantastic tale of Jesus Christ and the Stable of Promise.

PART FOUR

Narrator   There's no time to waste! Things are coming to a head! No magic wands to be waved, no charms and potions to be learned - simply someone full of wonder to be gazed upon. What is about to happen now in our tale will change the world forever! So, come now to witness the birth of Jesus Christ in the Stable of Promise.

Joseph and Innkeeper stand outside the stable looking in at Mary lying beside the crib.

Joseph   (*To Innkeeper*) He's so cute! So tiny! So perfect.

Innkeeper   They all are at that age.

Joseph	My mum said I looked like my dad when I was born. But then they turned me up the right way.
Innkeeper	How's your good lady doing? Is she coping? It's always a bit scary being presented with your first child - not to mention tiring!
Joseph	She's doing really well. Just having a bit of a doze while the wee one sleeps too.
Innkeeper	Good idea. You need to sleep when you can. *(Pointing to back of audience)* Looks like the peace is about to be shattered though.
Joseph	Who are they? Friends of yours?
Innkeeper	Just down off the hills by the look of them. Slightly merry too by the way they're weaving down the road, arms waving...
Joseph	Maybe they'll just keep going... walk right by... I'll just nip back into the barn and make sure Mary's Ok.

Joseph sits down by Mary and crib. Shepherds approach. Loud agitated discussions - 'You go first, no, you go' etc

Innkeeper	Now, now, gents, let's have a little shush round here. We've got a new baby who's just got off to sleep.
Shepherd 2	Right! That's it! This is stupid. I'm off.

Shepherd 2 turns to go but is pulled back by the others.

Shepherd 1	Sorry to bother you, Sir, but we'd like... we'd like...
Innkeeper	A good bottle of sherry?
Shepherd 3	No! No - what he means is we'd like... we'd like to...

Innkeeper   Order a couple of shandys!

Shepherd 2   Yes please! *(The others look at him)* I mean, no. *(Nudges others)* Why not?

Shepherd 1   Did you say you'd a new baby here?

Innkeeper   I did.

Shepherd 3   That's why we've come. Do you mind if we ask you where he is?

Innkeeper   Right behind me - in the barn. That's why I asked you to keep your voices down - don't want to wake the wee soul up, do we?

Shepherd 1   That's what we wanted to ask you - if you had a baby here, wrapped in swaddling clothes and lying in a manger?

Innkeeper   Are you friends of the family?

Shepherd 3   Not exactly...

Shepherd 2   Not exactly?! *(Looking at Shepherd 3)* Not exactly?! We've never met them in our lives!

Innkeeper   Then how did you know about the baby?

The 3 shepherds look at each other...

Shepherd 1   Let's just say some mutual friends told us about him.

Shepherd 2   *Sang* about him, in fact.

Innkeeper   *(Scratching head)* Look, I'm not quite sure what's going on here but the last thing Mary is going to want is you three tramping in with your big boots and your...

Shepherd 2   We'll take them off!

              Bends down to undo laces...

Innkeeper   And your smelly feet.

Shepherd 2   *(Stops and sniffs boot)* Phew! Maybe not...

              Puts boot back on.

Mary   *(Sitting up)* Let them come in.

Innkeeper   Are you sure, Ma'am?

Mary   Let them come in.

              *Shepherds go and stand beside Mary, Joseph and crib and
              kneel down. While Innkeeper watches them go in, the three
              Professors appear.*

Innkeeper   *(Looking at the family)* I don't suppose they carry any more
              germs than the animals whose hay he's sleeping in...

              Turns round - gets a fright when he sees the professors.

              Oh, my goodness! What a fright you gave me! Where did
              you three come from?

Professor 1   From the East.

Innkeeper   From Embra?3

Professor 3   The *far* East.

Professor 2   We come looking for a baby.

Innkeeper   You too? This is getting weird!

3 i.e. Edinburgh; or name the next big town to the east of you.

73

Professor 1   He's been talked about for centuries.

Professor 3   He's the one we've all been waiting for.

Professor 1   To rescue us.

Professor 3   To save us.

Professor 2   Although *he* doesn't know it yet.

Innkeeper   He doesn't know anything yet. He's too small.

Professor 2   We have presents for him.

Innkeeper   I hope it's something useful! I remember hearing a story once about a boy thought by some to be special and they gave him a wand, a cloak and an owl for presents - what use are those kinds of things to anyone? Mind you, it *was* just a story...

Professor 1   Ours are gifts that befit a very special and very real prince. Now can you direct us to the palace?

Innkeeper   The palace! A prince! He hasn't even got a tiny room under the stairs at his cousins - the baby is in the stable. Beside the animals. Just over here. *(Pointing)* And no doubt if she was happy to let three shepherds in she'll be happy enough to let you lot in too.

Professor 3   Lead on.

All four join the family. The three professors each give the baby their presents.

Narrator   *(In a David Attenborough whisper)* He's arrived! Safe and sound! No special mark on his forehead makes him stand out, but there in that crib, without the shadow of a doubt, lies the one baby who can save the world... *(Pause)* The real world... Jesus Christ in this stable, full now of promise...